Berkshire
Edited by Angela Fairbrace

First published in Great Britain in 2007 by:
Young Writers
Remus House
Coltsfoot Drive
Peterborough
PE2 9JX
Telephone: 01733 890066
Website: www.youngwriters.co.uk

All Rights Reserved

© Copyright Contributors 2007

SB ISBN 978-1 84431 111 8

Foreword

Young Writers was established in 1991 and has been passionately devoted to the promotion of reading and writing in children and young adults ever since. The quest continues today. Young Writers remains as committed to the nurturing of poetic and literary talent as ever.

This year's Young Writers competition has proven as vibrant and dynamic as ever and we are delighted to present a showcase of the best poetry from across the UK and in some cases overseas. Each poem has been selected from a wealth of *Little Laureates* entries before ultimately being published in this, our sixteenth primary school poetry series.

Once again, we have been supremely impressed by the overall quality of the entries we have received. The imagination, energy and creativity which has gone into each young writer's entry made choosing the poems a challenging and often difficult but ultimately hugely rewarding task - the general high standard of the work submitted ensured this opportunity to bring their poetry to a larger appreciative audience.

We sincerely hope you are pleased with this final collection and that you will enjoy *Little Laureates Berkshire* for many years to come.

Contents

Aldryngton Primary School
David Whelan (8)	1
Mina Tiwari (8)	2
Helena Grace Matheson (8)	3
Alex Cook (9)	4
Samantha Lee (7)	5
Thomas McIntyre (8)	6

Cranbourne Primary School
Scott Chamberlain (9)	7
Luke Cowley (9)	8
Krystal Smith (10)	9
Charley Bird (9)	10
Megan Clark (9)	11
George Maxwell (10)	12
Emily Harding (10)	13
Ella Manning (9)	14
Daniel Gordon (10)	15
Bethany Stevenson (10)	16
Andi-Louise Davidson (9)	17
Abbie Maddams (9)	18
Matthew Westbury (10)	19
Nicholas Baker (10)	20
Aaron Oliver (10)	21
Hilary Groves (10)	22
Madeline Chandler (9)	23
James Carter (9)	24
Harry Ledermann (10)	25
William Hardy (9)	26
Victoria Raistrick (9)	27
Tabitha Horsefield (10)	28
Miles Anderson (10)	29
Mathew Mansfield (10)	30

Dolphin School
Tobyn Nicholls (8)	31
Madeleine Panto (9)	32
Emma Mansell	33
Liam Cook (9)	34

Rosie Dart (9) — 35
Rowan Jade Eastabrook (9) — 36

Licensed Victuallers' School
Felix Johnston-Brunn (11) — 37
David Kempton (10) — 38
Juan Carlos Coral (11) — 39
Rhys Copeland (11) — 40
Jake Hodge (11) — 41
Ben Viney (11) — 42
Robyn Nixon (11) — 43
Kieran Smith (11) — 44
Niall Johnson (11) — 45
Elspeth Kinns (10) — 46
Lee O'Rourke (11) — 47
Kirsty Exley (10) — 48
Michaela Butler (11) — 49
Jeong Min Park (11) — 50
Sophie Pace (11) — 51
Lizzie Hamilton (9) — 52
Georgia Hawley (8) — 53
Matthew Rawlinson (8) — 54
Beth Appleton (9) — 55
Sara Hobbs (9) — 56
Ellen Jones (9) — 57
Oliver Smith (11) — 58
Marcus Tait (10) — 59
Divesh Prithviraj (10) — 60
Alex Kent (10) — 61
Kyra Sohns (11) — 62
Dominique Gilbert (10) — 63
Georgia Morrison (11) — 64
Madeleine Kinner (10) — 65
Jessica Cowell (10) — 66
Ben Jeffery (11) — 67
Zoë Carlin (9) — 68
Tanis Roberts-Clark (9) — 69
Robert Cheung (8) — 70
Ryan Murphy (8) — 71
Louise Rooker (9) — 72
Michael Taylor (10) — 73

Marlborough Primary School
Ronika Choudhury (10)	74
Reem Rafat (11)	75
Gowsaleya Sriskantharajah (11)	76
Charley Bhagat (10)	77
Lee Pelton (11)	78
Michelle Wong (10)	79
Angel Holmes (11)	80
Charlie Brough (10)	81
Olivia Megan Wheeldon (10)	82
Sofia Abdula (10)	83
Hodan Hassan (11)	84
Hayley Louise Wood (10)	85
Muhammad Mahmoud (11)	86
Lily Simone Cyphus (11)	87
Tega Akpoduado (10)	88
Paul Hutchings (10)	89
Cameron Knights (11)	90
Sahr Mian (11)	91
Nathan-Lee Scotts (11)	92
Holly Dawkins-Hirst (11)	93
James Hawes (11)	94
Tayo Foluso-Henry (10)	95
Jodie O'Farrell (10)	96
Sabrina Singh (10)	97
Joshua Scurville (10)	98
Ben Langham (10)	99
Rishi Sharma (11)	100
Emily-Rose Lucas (11)	101
Rosey Hogan Life (10)	102
Ryan Holmes (11)	103
Sabrina Sahota (10)	104
Jessica Bennett (10)	105
Maham Ijaz (11)	106

Our Lady of Peace RC Junior School
Emma Jade Flint (11)	107
Kayleigh Irwin (10)	108
Ben Buckley (10)	109
Heidi Lansley (11)	110
Georgina Irwin (10)	111

Adam Orr (10)	112
Cristina Lucci (10)	113
Joseph Allen (11)	114
Rajiv Vadher (10)	115
Matt Mault (11)	116
Parondeep Sandhu (10)	117
Christie Jeffries (11)	118
Rohan Wattley (11)	119
Beth Quarterman (10)	120
Alex Shaw (10)	121
Mary Porter (11)	122
Charlie Thomas (10)	123
Luke Thomas (11)	124
Samara Richardson (11)	125
Patrick Smyth (10)	126
Sophie Holder (11)	127
Toby Whatley (10)	128
Dominika Kwiatkowska (10)	129
Daniel Crouch (10)	130
Stefano Duarte Gouveia (11)	131
Oliver Hodge (10)	132
Fiona Hughes (11)	133
Daniela Ioviero (10)	134
Alice Kearley (11)	135
Waqar Shafi (11)	136
Dominika Krawczyk (10)	137
Oscar Ness (10)	138
Bethany Worth (11)	139
Luke Connor (11)	140
Ryan Stevens	141
Connor Swan (10)	142
Jake Wheatley (10)	143
Rochelle John (10)	144
Jack January (10)	145
Aaron Wetton (11)	146
Jack Tucker (10)	147
Hoisin Molloy (11)	148
Rhiannon Wood (11)	149
Laura Gotts (10)	150
Sam Wealleans (10)	151
Patrick Bart (10)	152
Chloe Park (10)	153

Jamie Crouch (10)	154
Charlie Watkins (11)	155
Liam Bibby (11)	156
Emma Johnston (11)	157
George Clark (10)	158
Sophie Boyce (10)	159
Sidonie Satchell (10)	160
Kamran Atwal (10)	161

Our Lady's Preparatory School

Sebastian Huddy (11)	162
Ben Cross (11)	163
Miguel O'Donnell (10)	164
Robin Fenlon (10)	165
Chantelle Brennan (11)	166
Luke Bainbridge (10)	167
Sammie Liu (10)	168
Matthew Prior (10)	169
Reuben O'Brien (11)	170

Radstock Primary School

Simran Birring (11)	171
Ammar Mohamed (11)	172
Sarah Taylor (10)	173
Anastasia Baker (10)	174
Zack Baddeley (11)	175
Daniel Peacock (11)	176
Kate Phillips (11)	177
Nico Vazquez-Oliveira (10)	178
Gemma Kinch (11)	179

Wessex Primary School

Sakshi Raizada (10)	180
Leah Collins (10)	181
Grace Perfect (9)	182
Katie Hawkins (9)	183
Daisy Fox (9)	184
Leyan Yucel (10)	185
Jennifer Barnard (9)	186
Megan Robson (10)	187
Alicia Carrington (9)	188

Louise Cockrell (9)	189
Shannon Bett (9)	190
Jack Brinsden (10)	191
Beni Grossman (9)	192
Matthew Sadlier (10)	193
Layla Haigh-Ellery (9)	194
Catherine Styles (10)	195

The Poems

A Dad Needs

A dad needs:
A deafening voice like an angry lion's roar,
A short temper like a tiny child,
A clever mind like a mad professor,
Arms like a strong Mr Universe,
Money like a wealthy celebrity,
Hair like an untidy rock artist,
Fashion like a clothes designer,
Slippers like my mum's fluffy ones,
A romantic touch like Cupid's strongest arrow.

David Whelan (8)
Aldryngton Primary School

A Squirrel

A squirrel has:
Eyes as black as night-time,
Ears as round as a goldfish bowl,
Fur as soft as snow,
And toes as pointy as sharp daggers.

A squirrel is:
As friendly as a wild bear,
As cute as a cuddly teddy bear,
As small as a pencil case.

Mina Tiwari (8)
Aldryngton Primary School

If . . .

If I were a kitten
I'd say,
'I'm looking for my mitten!'

If I were a footballer
I'd say,
'I wish I were taller!'

If I were a giraffe
I'd say,
'I need a very long scarf!'

If I were a bee
I'd say,
'Don't buzz around me!'

Helena Grace Matheson (8)
Aldryngton Primary School

What A Brain Needs

What a brain needs:

Logic like an instruction manual,
Memory like an old elephant,
Juices like burning acid,
Awareness like my puppy dog.

Alex Cook (9)
Aldryngton Primary School

If . . .

If I were a monkey
I'd say,
'I am very funky!'

If I were a bee
I'd say,
'Give me some money!'

If I were a moon
I'd say,
'See you very soon!'

If I were a fish
I'd say,
'Give me a kiss!'

If I were a panther
I'd say,
'My name is Samantha!'

Samantha Lee (7)
Aldryngton Primary School

If . . .

If I were a bee
I'd say,
'I want some money!'

If I were a flower
I'd say,
'I've got the power!'

If I were a cat
I'd say,
'I want a rat!'

If I were a fish
I'd say,
'*Argh!* Get me out of the dish!'

If I were a tree
I'd say,
'Get off me!'

Thomas McIntyre (8)
Aldryngton Primary School

Pirates

In a pirate's cabin with a wisp of smoke,
Sits the ragged old captain with holes in his clothes.
His razor-sharp iron sword would slit your throat,
Decaying old teeth shatter as he chews a bone.
His rotten wooden leg with woodworms growing in it.
His cruel, nasty parrot that pecks at you all day long.
The captain's eye patch covers an eye lost in a battle.
His skin so dirty it looks like he hasn't washed in years.
His black, greasy beard is as slimy as glue.
In his swaying cabin as the waves crash onto the boat.

Scott Chamberlain (9)
Cranbourne Primary School

Best Friend

My best friend is super funny when I am sad,
My best friend is as helpful as a circus clown,
My best friend is as helpful as a teacher in class,
My best friend is kind when I need something,
My best friend is fun when I go to his house,
My best friend is enthusiastic when we play a game,
My best friend is silly when I am unhappy,
My best friend is always smiling at school,
My best friend is cheerful, like a clown,
My best friend is confident when we play football,
My best friend is co-operative when we play 'It',
My best friend is friendly when we are at school,
My best friend is fair when we play basketball,
My best friend is always laughing at my jokes,
My best friend is thoughtful when we play games,
My best friend is strong when he gets told off,
My best friend is joyful when we go for a break,
My best friend is *sooooo* cool!

Luke Cowley (9)
Cranbourne Primary School

My Best Friend

My best friend ever,
She giggles like a hyena,
She is kind and caring,
She is as funny as a clown,
She has pretty long blonde hair,
She has crystal-blue eyes,
She is as pretty as a princess.

She is as happy as a hippo having a mud bath,
She is as challenging as a man jumping from a plane,
My best friend will be my best friend forever,
Wherever we are, we are still best friends.
My friend will always be my best friend.

Krystal Smith (10)
Cranbourne Primary School

My Friend

My friend has:
Hair as long as a broomstick,
Eyes as wide as the Nile,
A wart as big as a muddy puddle,
And ears as big as an elephant's.

Cheeks as circular as Hula Hoops,
A nose as big as a tiger's head,
Teeth as sharp as a knife,
And a chin as chubby as a pig's bottom.

And that's just the way I like him!

Charley Bird (9)
Cranbourne Primary School

Friends

My super best friend is so silly,
She is like a clown doing somersaults.
My friend is always friendly,
When I'm sad she cheers me up.
My friend is helpful,
Like a nurse looking after others.
My friend is thoughtful,
When you're lonely she'll come to you.
My friend is ticklish,
Like a hyena laughing.
My friend is calm,
Like when you go to bed and dream.
My friend is always happy,
She has a big smile on her face.
My friend is fun,
She thinks of good games.
My friend is kind,
She shares her toys with me.
My friend is funny,
She makes me happy and cheerful.
My friend is cool,
She always has funky clothes.
Oh, what a friend!

Megan Clark (9)
Cranbourne Primary School

Aliens

One night a light was blocked out,
So I went downstairs to see
If it was an octopus
Or a giant bumblebee!

As I tiptoed down the stairs,
My head was spinning around,
I knew I was not wrong,
For I heard a dreadful sound!

The alien was scared,
It quickly ran away.
I would have seen it a little longer
But my parents shouted, 'Hey!'

And the alien ran away . . .

George Maxwell (10)
Cranbourne Primary School

Ahoy There!

Ahoy, ahoy, now what do I see?
Pirates with parrots
And sharks in the sea.

Pirates are mean, pirates are scary,
They are tough
And very hairy.

The captain has a very long beard,
A great long jacket
And he is very weird.

He likes to say, 'Walk the plank'
And 'Clean the decks,'
And ties his ship up on a bank.

The waves splash and crash
When it is night,
Thunder roars and lightning flashes.

Ahoy, ahoy, now what did you find?
I hope this poem has put a lot in your mind.

Emily Harding (10)
Cranbourne Primary School

The Scary Monster

Last night I had a dream,
I saw a monster in my basement.
It was black with red spots,
Had six eyes, six legs, two arms
And a hundred teeth.

He ate *children!*
He picked them up
Nibbled their heads
And gobbled the rest!

He let out a big bellow
Then chased after me.
A dead end!
I was alarmed,
Shivering all over,
Knees knocking.

He stared down at me,
Drooling from the mouth.
I screamed . . .
And woke up!

Ella Manning (9)
Cranbourne Primary School

My Best Friend And Me

My best friend is a mate who is kind,
We are always together, he never minds,
We love playing in football tournaments,
Against all our other friends.

My best friend is like my brother,
We've been friends since we were small,
When we play together, I have to smile,
I hope we'll be friends until we die.

He has a little brother and great parents,
We play for a brilliant football team,
I play up front, he's in defence,
We hope we'll be famous one day.

Most of all we are great friends,
We love working together in class,
We sit next to each other at lunch,
We really are best friends.

Daniel Gordon (10)
Cranbourne Primary School

Dreams

A dream, a dream is full of light,
They are usually good, they don't give you a fright,
They can be of a field with a flock of sad sheep,
Or of a very old map and treasure to keep.

One dream was full of cross fairies,
Another had yellow canaries,
Some have pirates and sailing ships,
Others have men with mouths of zips.

Dreams can be at any time,
If you're cooking or cleaning up grime,
They're make-believe in your head,
So don't believe what the characters said.

In conclusion, I feel a dream is a dream,
If they are in the sun or a moonbeam,
A dream, a dream is full of light,
They are usually good, they don't give you a fright.

Bethany Stevenson (10)
Cranbourne Primary School

My Alien

My alien lives in a big green field,
With no one to see him,
No one to hug;
People are scared of him,
People have nightmares about him.

He's so scary - he's got one big eye,
And four arms that flop around,
And two fat fingers
That sizzle like sausages,
And he moves like jelly on a stick.

But that's my alien.

Andi-Louise Davidson (9)
Cranbourne Primary School

Best Friend

When I'm feeling down she comes to see me,
She supports me when I'm being bullied,
She has a lovely brother and
Some of the kindest parents I know.

She has brown hair, hazel eyes,
And a beautiful smile,
But best of all she has
A caring and magnificent heart.

She's always smiling
Like a child on their birthday,
She's the moon and sun to make me happy,
And she's my best friend!

Abbie Maddams (9)
Cranbourne Primary School

Smelly Nelly

There once was a boy called Nelly,
Who was disgustingly smelly,
His mum wanted him to have a bath
But Nelly thought she was having a laugh.

Every day Nelly went to school
Where he thought he was very cool,
They all thought he was very ugly,
But his mum believed he was just snugly.

Each day Smelly Nelly flew home,
Whizzing along in a flying gnome,
But when he got there his mum was gone,
He didn't understand what was going on.

Upstairs he found a big bath full of bubbles,
Then he knew his day was full of troubles
His mum was waiting with a bath,
She really was not having a laugh.

Poor Nelly!

Matthew Westbury (10)
Cranbourne Primary School

Alien

Green and slimy,
Five arms covered in goo,
One leg as bumpy as a hill,
He smelt like a loo.

He picked up a stone and ate it,
The holes in his head were ears,
He twitched as he walked,
And burst into tears.

He had one big eye
And was made from jelly,
He was very shy
And extremely smelly.

He had one disgusting finger,
He was shiny with slime,
And his breath smelt like vinegar,
Then he was lost in time.

Nicholas Baker (10)
Cranbourne Primary School

Aliens

An alien, even worse than you think.

He had six bloodshot eyes,
Even four crinkly ears,
He had five wobbly legs
And three muscled arms.

He was shining blue
And red-chequered,
He had one thin antenna,
And was even half pig.

He had his eyes
On his big tummy,
He had his ears
On his wobbly legs.

He stole my helmet,
I was struggling to breathe,
He stole my ray gun,
He aimed it at me.

He shot and he hit
The alien behind me,
I had to go back
In my magical spaceship.

An alien, even worse than you think.

Aaron Oliver (10)
Cranbourne Primary School

Pirates

My pirate is Captain Curly Hair,
And he was a brilliant pirate,
With an eye patch and a fierce eye,
His crew was as thick as planks.

He wished to kidnap the princess of Spain,
With a parrot called PG who was blue and yellow,
The echo of his loud bellow filled the land,
He could never swim so he used armbands.

Curly Hair never failed his tasks,
The ship had a huge mast,
He smelt like skunk and kangaroo sweat,
Had a monkey as a buddy and pet.

Hilary Groves (10)
Cranbourne Primary School

Pirates!

Pirates, pirates, here they come,
Singing, laughing and drinking rum.

Buckled straps on belted shoes,
So hide yourself or die - you choose.

Long braided hair and eye patches too,
Mutiny, treachery and a hullabaloo.

Walk the plank, dig for treasure,
Meeting their parrots is always a pleasure.

Every captain needs a crew,
To guide them over the seas so blue.

They pull up the anchor and hoist the sails,
Then sit by the side and greet the whales.

Pirates, pirates, they're mean and scary,
We're warning you - they're very hairy.

Lock up your doors, safe and tight,
Pirates will be here tonight.

Madeline Chandler (9)
Cranbourne Primary School

Weird Noises

What's that noise banging down there?
What are they doing? Who is there?
What's that I can see?
Aliens drinking their bubbly tea!

On no, what are they doing?
Phew, they're only eating their pudding.
They're getting closer, getting nearer,
I can see them now much clearer.

How do they look?
Wormy hair and four eyes, too.
Now I can see them, what will they do?
I think it's time to go, don't you?

James Carter (9)
Cranbourne Primary School

The Deadly Pirates

The deadly pirates are so *drunk*
On the sailing ship,
The daft, dumb pirates are so *rude*
Whenever they speak to each other.

They look with their one *eye*
When they look for enemies,
They always *snore* loudly,
Sleeping in their hammocks.

Their cannons are so loud,
They're deaf in one *second,*
The *rude* parrot always swears,
Copying the drunken pirates.

Harry Ledermann (10)
Cranbourne Primary School

A Dream Day

Skiing, sledging every day,
Everybody is in the sleigh,
Skidding down, climbing up,
Lots of people getting stuck.

Off we go to the ice rink,
Ooh, now I'm turning pink,
We have had such fun,
Come on, it's time for a cream bun.

Come on now, let's go home,
Mum, can we have an ice cream cone?
No, my dears, it's time for bed,
But Mum, I've got a throbbing head!

What a dream day!

William Hardy (9)
Cranbourne Primary School

Alien Party

What are they doing?
Dinosaurs, spiders, mutant beasts,
Well, they are having a feast.

What's on the table?
Why, I'll go and see,
Eyeballs, frogs and mouldy tea.

What do they look like?
Now give me a sec,
Forty sharp teeth and a very long neck.

Now that's not all,
A fat belly too,
Spaghetti hair and spit like dew.

What is it like?
You may very well ask,
Dark and gloomy, what a task.

Oh, my goodness!
Well, I'll tell you what now,
I've been swallowed, I don't know how.

How will I get out?
How will I get free?
How will I live and again be me?

Victoria Raistrick (9)
Cranbourne Primary School

Pleckley's Adventure

Pleckley was space-wrecked on Plair,
The country was deserted, nothing there.
He lived in a cave on a hill,
And any visitors, he tried to kill!

He found an alien's designer top,
But he came up to a stop,
And out of a pot he found a squid,
And gobbled that up he did.

He fell into a black hole,
And in there he found a mole,
He lived in a turnip,
He then tried hard to burn it.

But he failed his task,
And instead got killed extremely fast.

Tabitha Horsefield (10)
Cranbourne Primary School

Pirates

I sail the seas in my boat
And all my friends call me Cut Throat,
I have a big black beard and lace at my chin
And I stay up all night drinking gin.

While we're looking for treasure, digging in the dirt,
I have black leather boots and a frilly shirt,
I have a huge black hat and a parrot at my side,
We search the land for treasure to hide.

We sail the seas in stormy weather,
We steal from other boats for our pleasure,
We shoot our giant cannons into the sky,
For I am a pirate, now you know why.

Miles Anderson (10)
Cranbourne Primary School

Aliens

Aliens are green and gross,
But this one is the worst;
It is as big as a spaceship,
And it doesn't need fresh air.

It has spikes on its arms,
And its blood is coloured sky-blue,
Its skin is coloured the deepest red,
And it has hard black scales all over, too.

It has five long arms with hands on, too,
Make sure that they don't get you,
It has two long legs,
And four axe-shaped wings.

So, if you're out at night, peer in the dark,
And watch out, for it might be near,
And if you are out in space,
Make sure your shuttle is stable.

It'll be waiting.

Mathew Mansfield (10)
Cranbourne Primary School

Spring

Trees bursting from the deep winter slumber,
these ancient trees festooned with too many buds to number.

Bursting up through the canopy of dropped leaves
comes a spike of green, purple and white.

The shadow of the forest is unravelled
by this new source of light.

Deep underground lies a brown ball of fur,
the first sign of spring is when a dormouse will stir.

He scampers and scurries around this new place,
happy once again to be back in his own space.

Tobyn Nicholls (8)
Dolphin School

Summer To Winter

Summer

Summery feelings,
Summery day,
Dazzling butterflies heading my way,
I feel like a king in his castle on his throne,
All the wonderfully colourful flowers lean,
And the breeze is almost a moan,
I'm walking through paradise when I'm in my garden
On my own.

Winter

The winter fire burning bright,
The winter weather howling in fright,
All but one is out tonight,
The howling wind,
Evil mist and snow,
I look from the warmth
Onto a white winter world.

Madeleine Panto (9)
Dolphin School

Wintry Poem

Conditions are icy
dazzling breakdown
a surprising crash
a foggy temperature
an Arctic freeze
Expose your anorak
and your scarf
blizzard breaks to zero
then a damp cough
hailstones petrify
anxious people let out a scream
frozen hands put on gloves
frozen heads put on hats
centigrade turns to zero
lots of people get hypothermia
think of the people in Antarctica
freezing to death.

Emma Mansell
Dolphin School

Football!

Football is great, football is fun,
Football is great when the strikers run,
When it's a draw and the penalties come,
The players are happy like they've just won.

Football is a passion,
Who cares about fashion?
Mostly it's men who cheer when they score,
So all I can hear is a big, loud roar!

Liam Cook (9)
Dolphin School

Candy World

There's a sweetie as tall as the door,
And liquorice as long as the floor!

The ceiling is basically cocoa,
If there were any vegetables I'd say 'No, no.'

The rain is made of Dolly Mix,
There are lollipops that everyone licks.

In the park there's a huge chocolate fountain,
And in the countryside there's an ice cream mountain.

I'd love to live in a place like this,
But my friend who eats greens says, 'Give it a miss!'

Rosie Dart (9)
Dolphin School

Jelly Bean Café

The Jelly Bean Café by the riverside
Is full of lovely fun and colourful beans,
In the Jelly Bean Café by the riverside
Nothing is as it seems.

In the Jelly Bean Café by the riverside,
All you ever eat are *jelly beans!*
The jelly bean trees by the riverside
Are tastier than anything!

Rowan Jade Eastabrook (9)
Dolphin School

The Shark's Tale

Oh, why do you fear me?
Is it my size?
Is it my teeth?

It's not my fault
you dress like seals!
I may look like a brute
but that's just how I was made!

You may think I kill anything
and everything
but I'm just doing
what my ancestors have done!

I may have a gruesome reputation
but really I just want to be left alone.
If you think I am petrifying,
just imagine how I must be feeling!

Felix Johnston-Brunn (11)
Licensed Victuallers' School

Doggie's Despair

I sit alone all day,
Neglected by them,
Nothing to do or play,
I just sit here all day.

My life is a misery,
I live in a world of deceit,
You'll be all right,
You'll be okay,
They all lie to me.

I wish I could run away,
To some faraway place,
With someone to love and someone to hold,
So this is why I'm in despair,
All I ask for is a little love,
Do you not care?

David Kempton (10)
Licensed Victuallers' School

The Jumping Dolphin

An image of happiness.
Always smiling on the outside.
Inward sadness comes to me too.
Catching us with tuna,
Getting chased by sharks
Hurts me.
I am very friendly,
I like to jump out of the water,
Eating fish too.
Getting caught for shows
Horrifies me,
But I end up liking it.
I get mistaken for a shark,
But I save humans,
I like it when people cheer.
If you are enjoying yourself, remember us,
The jumping dolphins.

Juan Carlos Coral (11)
Licensed Victuallers' School

The Polar Bear's Plea

Day by day they take us away,
Shipping us to our doom.
Who are they?
None of us know.
Where do they live?
I don't know.
Why do they want us?
What have we done?
We do not deserve this torture.
Why are we on the 'extinction' list?
They prod us, poke us and make us sad.
That's what they do, they make us sad.
Now it's my turn, here comes the net.
They've got me.
I'm being beaten and tortured . . .
They've locked me up in a block of captivity,
Surrounded by them, hundreds of them, thousands of them.
They also love my fur.
They find it comfy and warm,
All I'm asking for is to be *free!*

Rhys Copeland (11)
Licensed Victuallers' School

Help The House Fly

Humans think it's funny hitting me with a stick,
But all I really want to do is get out,
Even though all you do is hit me,
Hit me till I die,
I try to get out but there's something in the way,
And all you big people do is smack me,
Smash me, swipe me.
So please next time you see me, let me out
And I will fly away free, happy and thankful.

Jake Hodge (11)
Licensed Victuallers' School

The Blue Whale

I am nearly extinct.
Although I am the biggest mammal,
I am the friendliest mammal.
But that's not what you think.
You humans think that I am an evil monster,
But you are the monsters as you kill me and then eat me.

You are cruel, careless people,
You pollute the water in which I live and breathe.
I have to try and survive breathing in all that fuel and gas.
All I eat is krill, do I harm you?

You don't like me, you never have.
You think of me as a waste of space.
If only I had a voice.

Ben Viney (11)
Licensed Victuallers' School

Waiting Wolves

Cold in the snow
Whistling noises from the wind through my fur
Bang, bang, bang!
The gunshots go again
Every night without fail they come
Our homes are destroyed
We are left wandering in the snow
Why is it our fur they want?
My mother is there through the trees
I have found her at last, I can see her tail
Then I notice her tail on their head
My son is horrified
He gets so scared
Just so scared.

Robyn Nixon (11)
Licensed Victuallers' School

Tiger's Explanation

You think I'm scary, a brutal creature, but I'm not.
You think I eat anything, but it's only food for my family.
On the inside, I'm a soft cat, but that's not what the hunters see.
For them I'm a target where they win my coat and my sharp teeth.
I'm scared to sleep each night. Each day my family gets smaller.
Why can't you leave me alone?
I'm running through the fields, so scared I won't stop.

Kieran Smith (11)
Licensed Victuallers' School

Elephants Never Forget

I am lonely, very lonely,
An orphan, that's what I am,
Through no fault of my own.
Mum died in front of me,
Thrashing and trumpeting,
And then, that bang.
I was one month old,
Didn't know what it meant,
It was about to change my life.

I charged, trumpeting feebly,
Men started laughing
And poking me.
I darted away into the bush.
I often visit this place,
Don't know why, just emotions.

Niall Johnson (11)
Licensed Victuallers' School

The Deer's Despair

Do they think I like dying?
Well I don't!
I like running free in the forest, eating leaves, and now,
                              the last of my family gone.
Imagine if you were me and I killed you, would you care then?
Please don't take my head and hang it on a wall!
Do you ever dream that there are human skin handbags?
I wouldn't buy one.
You don't need this fur, it's mine!
I would love to prance in peace on a bright, brilliant and beautiful day.
Leave us alone in this calm world, please!

Elspeth Kinns (10)
Licensed Victuallers' School

A Dolphin's Life

Diving under the sea.
You don't think much of me!
Probably you just like me for my tricks.
Sharks look at me, they think they will beat me,
But they're wrong, *smash, crack,* and there,
Down, down, they float, one by one.
You try to kill me for my meat,
Sometimes you capture me from up high by nets, it's horrible!
I try to help others but I am mistaken because of my back fin.
It's unfair.

Lee O'Rourke (11)
Licensed Victuallers' School

A Donkey's Distress

I plod along,
For me it's a never-ending walk up the same old beach,
Sand blows into my eyes,
Water soaks my ears,
I long to be free,
But you humans don't,
You call me a coward,
But I can be as brave as a lion,
I can fight off anyone or anything that wants to challenge me,
If you would just give me a chance.
Why am I hated?
What is wrong with me?
I just want to be loved.

Kirsty Exley (10)
Licensed Victuallers' School

Little Badger

Why are you people so mean?
What did we do to you?
You kill us.
It's not fair.

You set traps.
All we do is run and hide,
Then all of a sudden one more of us is dead.

We struggle to survive.
We lose our families.
It's not like anyone cares.
We also have feelings too.

We only come out at night.
It's the safest time.
We still die.
Our stripes look like the road,
Then we get run over.

Our one wish is that you will leave.
Leave us alone.

Michaela Butler (11)
Licensed Victuallers' School

The Penguin's Plea

Stuck in the frosty, cold Antarctica,
Waiting for someone to come and listen to me,
Understand me, save me.
Most of my family and friends were hunted by humans
Who destroyed our habitat.
Antarctica was a home to me before the humans came.
Will anyone understand my feelings?

Antarctica is a habitat for animals
But humans are destroying the wildlife.
Oil spills are ruining our home
I can't watch them do this.
How would they like it if we did this to them?
Are all humans like this?
Antarctica is freezing in sorrow with the other penguin colonies
Who don't want their homes destroyed.

What have we done to you to make you so angry?
We are innocent animals.
You own something that we don't own
Something that makes you feel like you can do anything you like.
Freedom!
Freedom is what I want.
Freedom is what we all want.
You probably don't know how fortunate you are to have it
But I'd trade anything for that.

Jeong Min Park (11)
Licensed Victuallers' School

The Orca's Story

You silly humans think you're all-powerful,
But you're not, you just have a choice,
You can choose to let me be wild and free and stay in my element,
Instead you capture and enslave me,
Keeping me in tiny tanks I can barely turn around in,
Please at least give me a home and room to play in, please.

In the wild, I'm almost invincible,
But you and I fight a battle that isn't fair,
Making me like a hedgehog; a bundle of fear,
Actually I'm a coward, unable to fight back,
So when I'm starving, hungry, the last thing I want to see
Is your boat coming to take yet another of us away.

Once upon a time I was respected, even feared.
Then you would play with my cousins but never me,
What did I care though? You left me alone and that is all I wanted,
Now you kill me, hunt me, enslave me, take away my family
                                  and my cousins,
Those gentle creatures you used to play with,
They, too, are dragged away from home.

I've heard of cruelty and suffering,
I've heard of fear and pain,
But never have I heard of a member of my family being content
                                  with you,
What we are is what makes us strong, but what you make,
                                  makes you strong,

So maybe it is not you we should fear, it's what you make.
Maybe once you've heard this tale, this plea,
That is my story, my tale,
You'll gain some respect for me,
And the other creatures of the sea.

Sophie Pace (11)
Licensed Victuallers' School

I Wish I Were A . . .

I wish I were a cheetah that was slowish,
An ant that was biggish,
A fire that was coldish,
An ogre that was stylish,
A blue that was yellowish,
I wish I were an adult that was childish,
I wish I were a rhino that was softish,
A cube that was roundish.

Lizzie Hamilton (9)
Licensed Victuallers' School

Bunny Rabbit

A sharp clawer
A finger nibbler
A toe biter
A nose twitcher
A hungry eater
A fast escaper
An excellent hopper
A wonderful listener
A carrot chomper
A rain hater
A quick sprinter
A water drinker
A fur grower.

Georgia Hawley (8)
Licensed Victuallers' School

Who Am I?

Super spoiler,
Burning rubber,
Garage sleeper,
Swift hunter,
Vindictive driver,
Key turner,
Track racer,
Gas guzzler,
Road runner,
Two seater,
Gear changer,
Smoke blower.

Matthew Rawlinson (8)
Licensed Victuallers' School

A Friend

A great presenter
A clever thinker
An excellent player
A secret keeper
A problem solver
A memory maker
A kind carer
A constant comforter.

Beth Appleton (9)
Licensed Victuallers' School

Tree

A steady swayer
A grape grower
A monkey minder
A forest filler
A water wanter
A snow-day stripper
A paper producer
A lumberjack loather
A blossom bearer.

Sara Hobbs (9)
Licensed Victuallers' School

Teddy

A gentle cuddler,
A wonderful hugger,
Couldn't be nicer,
A cosy comforter,
A sound sleeper,
A caring companion,
A pyjama partner,
A bedtime bringer.

Ellen Jones (9)
Licensed Victuallers' School

The Rat's Side Of The Story

I am as hungry as the world's fattest pig.
I may be a rat but don't hate me, please love me like my best friend who lives in your warm loving home.

All of us have a natural craving for food.
We all look for a safe home like my family and I do.
We live in danger of your cats.

I would love a home with food and humans who respect us.

Don't be scared of me, I am as soft as your favourite cuddly toy and as loyal as man's best friend.

Everyone needs a friend as I am sure you do too.
So do my family and I.

Oliver Smith (11)
Licensed Victuallers' School

The Shark's Tale

Everyone fears me, although I want to be friendly
However my super-sharp teeth scare everyone away.

I don't kill everything, I only kill to live and feed my young.
I'm thought of as a big, brutal beast by you humans.
Also I am used in films to scare people when I try not to be scary.
Whenever someone gets cut, you scream, 'Shark, shark!'
When it is only a rock.

I may be a killing machine, but I don't kill everything I see.
So, if you are feeling lonely, think of me who doesn't have anyone!

Marcus Tait (10)
Licensed Victuallers' School

The Anaconda's Path

I am not too happy.
With the humans who want to kill me,
I can't live without the fear of being murdered.
But I cannot starve either,
I need to eat something.

I do not want to be harmful,
And I want to live with the other animals in peace.
However, they think I am too violent and bloodthirsty.
I am also different from the others,
Because I haven't got any bones.
Not even a single one in my body.
I don't even have arms or legs,
The only things I have are a dangerous head,
A venomous tail and a slithery body.

When I don't eat food there is a high chance I may starve.
I would like to stay like the other animals,
But I am stuck like this.

Divesh Prithviraj (10)
Licensed Victuallers' School

The Shark's Wish

My wish is to be loved,
Think of me all on my own, drifting, hoping,
But I don't know why,
I just think you are afraid of me,
I may look scary but I am just looking for happiness.
Is that too much to ask?

I do hate being on my own,
I have never been loved - probably never will be,
I never ever would hurt an animal - except for food.
I kill people because I think they are seals.

So that is me,
I only want love - please look after me,
That is my wish, but with my tail as long as a boat,
My wish may haunt me, I don't know.

Alex Kent (10)
Licensed Victuallers' School

Ranking Rats

I scurry along the attic of your house
You don't understand me
I only do what's good for me
But then you'll kill me with pesticides!

Some of you think I'm nasty
That I bring the plague
All I do is hunt for food
Is that such a crime?

Not all rats have fleas
I don't - I am a house rat
You must be kind
Don't stamp your feet on my back
Don't wait for me to die
I only do what's best for me.

You run away
And stand on chairs
I do not like living in fear
It's such a horrible wait
For someone to come and rescue me.

Kyra Sohns (11)
Licensed Victuallers' School

The Dolphin's Tale

You may think I'm a dancing dolphin, but no,
I am full of fear, meanwhile I catch my prey, looking out for predators.

My sharp beak is like a stick, my conical teeth like cones.
I have smooth skin like a pack of perfect peaches
and I am extremely intelligent.
Perhaps you have watched a film and laughed at my ludicrous beak.
You may feel that I'm happy but with those prickling predators
around me, there's a hundred percent chanting chance they'll come
                                                                                            after me.
Please believe me, I really do exist.
Under the waves and splashes of the ocean, there lives me.

Dominique Gilbert (10)
Licensed Victuallers' School

The Skunk's Tale

I've only ever been alone
I don't understand why
Every night I cry and cry
And think *why am I alive?*

I don't think I'm ugly,
In fact I think I'm quite beautiful.
I have black and white-coated fur,
Eyes as blue as the morning sky
And a magnificent voice like a hummingbird.
But when I elegantly lift my tail
Nobody but me is there,
I look around in amazement.
Was it something I said?

I try to talk to the rabbits
But they hop away.
I try to talk to the hedgehogs
But they curl up into a protective ball
And when I try to talk to the tortoises,
They run away faster than they ever have run before.

I suppose I will have to be alone for my lifetime,
So when you're feeling alone, think about me
And how my life is friendless.
Hey, what's that smell?

Georgia Morrison (11)
Licensed Victuallers' School

A Lion's Life

I stand there, king of the jungle.
Watching my prey, I leap! to catch my dinner.
My mane is as furry as a soft, comfortable rug.

Ragged fur mane being blown about in the wind,
I watch and take everything I see.

It may look like I'm tough
But I'm terrified of you poachers and hunters.

All I ask is for you to just leave me safe and free in my own world;
This world is large enough for us both.

Madeleine Kinner (10)
Licensed Victuallers' School

The Spider's Secrets

I crawl away quickly from my enemies,
Some think I am the enemy,
Though I am more scared of you, than you are of me.

I am black like the sky at night,
Hairy like a gorilla.
I lay my eggs in the warmth,
But you, you people, step on me,
Kill me without a second thought.

I have eight legs and you humans have two.
I will run around your neck
And you will feel a pinch of anger from me.

I dart across my web,
It is sticky but I cope,
Cope with my oily body.

I am a carnivore like every other spider.
I catch moths and flies,
Not with my hands or feet,
But my precious web.

So next time you see me,
Think of the terror you bring before it is too late.

Jessica Cowell (10)
Licensed Victuallers' School

The Cheetah's Way

Through the heat haze I watch you,
you don't know I'm there.
My piercing orange eyes follow your movements,
but still I am silent.

My cubs yelp, I must feed them,
I am watching their meal.
Speed is my advantage,
you don't stand a chance.

I accelerate towards you,
I see your ears prick up.
I *pounce,* and my claws hold on tight.
I am very sorry but my cubs are hungry.
They need to eat.
My cubs will feed well tonight.

You may think this is wrong,
you may think this is cruel,
but believe me, if you want your children to live,
you have to go that extra mile.

Ben Jeffery (11)
Licensed Victuallers' School

The Door
(Inspired by 'The Door' by Miroslav Holub)

Go and open the door,
Maybe outside there's an owl as swift as an ocean,
With feathery wings like lush emerald grass.

Go and open the door,
Maybe someone is creeping behind you,
Or he could be waiting to jump on you.

Go and open the door,
If there is rain pouring down,
The glowing sun will soon appear.

Go and open the door,
Even if there is nothing,
Even if you don't feel good,
Go and open the door.

At least you'll see the world outside!

Zoë Carlin (9)
Licensed Victuallers' School

The Door
(Inspired by 'The Door' by Miroslav Holub)

Go and open the door,
Maybe there is a panther
Sneaking through the immense jungle
Like a black rogue.

Go and open the door,
Maybe it will just be black
Or it may be yellow and red
Like a fire in the sky.

Go and open the door,
Maybe you will see something amusing
Or maybe something you hate
Like Mondays or sprouts.

Go and open the door,
Maybe you will see a Ferrari
As red as a garnet ring
Go and open the door.

At least you will have a new car.

Tanis Roberts-Clark (9)
Licensed Victuallers' School

The Door
(Inspired by 'The Door' by Miroslav Holub)

Go and open the door,
Maybe there will be a stripy tiger,
Tree, garden or sea.

Go and open the door,
It might be black,
Green, red or blue,
Like a planet spinning in the sky.

Go and open the door,
Maybe you'll see something missing
In the cold, dingy night.

Go and open the door,
Maybe you'll see a Porsche
As silver as a shiny coin.

At least you'll know what it's like to be outside.

Robert Cheung (8)
Licensed Victuallers' School

The Door
(Inspired by 'The Door' by Miroslav Holub)

Go and open the door,
Maybe there's a dog that clucks,
Or a jungle with no animals.

Go and open the door,
Maybe there's a chicken that's green,
Or a clown that doesn't make you laugh.

Go and open the door,
Maybe there's a motorway
Without any cars.

Go and open the door,
Maybe there's a tree as soft as a pillow
Or a cheetah as slow as a snail.

Go and open the door,
At least there will be a garden.

Ryan Murphy (8)
Licensed Victuallers' School

The Door
(Inspired by 'The Door' by Miroslav Holub)

Go and open the door,
Maybe there's a war like a terrifying thunderstorm,
Charging towards you,
Or a planet being destroyed
Like a tiny ant being crushed.

Go and open the door,
Maybe there's a dog with a pleading face
Waiting to play,
Or dazzling colours whirling around.

Go and open the door,
Maybe there's a horse galloping happily,
Or an instrument playing loudly.

Go and open the door,
At least there will be a smile.

Louise Rooker (9)
Licensed Victuallers' School

Rhinos

You might think I'm a weapon of destruction
But I am more frightened than you.
Visiting the savannah you think you're in danger,
Well so you might be but I am in more danger.
Hiding behind trees though I'm always spotted.
Like you I would prefer it if you leave me alone.
You are the dangerous monsters in the savannah.
Why do you come?
I can't escape easily yet you killed my family.
We are dying because you are shooting us,
On the very brink of extinction.
We need good Samaritans to help us.
Why can't you understand we are peaceful creatures?
It's you who is the bringer of annihilation.

Michael Taylor (10)
Licensed Victuallers' School

Snow Delight

The snow is like
Glittery sugar
Sprinkled on
Our face.

The snow is like
Crunchy crisps
Crunching under
Our feet.

The snow is like
Cream which gives
A glittery dream
To the children.

The awe-inspiring snow
Gives me a breath of fresh air.
The snow is glowing
Like a torch in the dark.

The children
Playing snow fights
Make other children
Full of delight.

Ronika Choudhury (10)
Marlborough Primary School

Snow

Snow falling on the trees,
In the cold, thick winter breeze.

Tears of joy falling down my cheeks,
My face filled with glee.

Blinded by the snow so white,
Floating in the air quite bright.

Soft, smooth snow as silent as a tiny mouse.

It is sugar spilling out of the jar,
Icing being spread on a cake.

Walking in the winter wonderland, running faster
And faster through the white sand.

It is a white blanket covering the houses,
Cars, roads and pavements.

Crystal snowflakes swirling round and round
And then drifting to the ground.

Reem Rafat (11)
Marlborough Primary School

Winter Snow

Snow is white as milk,
And as smooth as silk.

Snow falls down lightly like cotton,
As children make snow angels with their bottom.

Snow is white as milk,
And as smooth as silk.

My crisps are very munchy,
But the snow is even crunchy.

Snow is white as milk,
And as smooth as silk.

Watching children play with snow,
As it falls down very slow.

Snow is white as milk,
And as smooth as silk.

Some children inside watching Snow White,
As they don't want to get wet in the snowball fight.

Snow is white as milk,
And as smooth as silk.

Gowsaleya Sriskantharajah (11)
Marlborough Primary School

Snowy Days

Snow is like a wintertime wonderland,
And when you walk through it,
It goes *crunch, crunch.*

Snow is like a white bed sheet or
A football pitch covered in cream.

Moonlight snow falling from the sky,
Make sure your dreams come alive.

Snow looks like sprinkled sugar,
And a huge egg without the yolk.

Making snowmen is the best,
And it makes life so much fun.

Charley Bhagat (10)
Marlborough Primary School

Snow

I was playing in the snow.
Snow!
Snow is very cold.
Snow!
Snow is like egg without the yolk.
Snow!
Snow is like icing on a cake.
Snow!
Snow is like white bed sheets.
Snow!
Snow is like sugar.
Snow!

Lee Pelton (11)
Marlborough Primary School

Winter Snow

Winter is as cold as a
Freezing cold fridge.

Snow is a creamy fluffy sugar
People eat strawberries.

When you stride on the snow,
It goes *crunch, crunch.*

Snow is a silky white sand
for making sandcastles.

Children like building snowmen
And it creates joy.

When it snows all over,
It's like a spectacular world!

Michelle Wong (10)
Marlborough Primary School

The Snow

The snow is an egg without the yolk
It comes like sugar
The snow is soft like fluff
The paper is cut up in a thousand pieces
It smells fresh
The snow brings memories.

Angel Holmes (11)
Marlborough Primary School

Snow!

Snow is icing on a cake.
Snow!
Snow is an explosion in a cloud factory.
Snow!
Snow is a winter wonderland.
Snow!
Snow brings back nice memories of childhood.
Snow!
Snow is a football pitch covered in cream.
Snow!
Snow is an egg without the yolk.
Snow!
Snow is frozen milk.
Snow!
Snow is a blank sheet of paper.
Snow!
Snow is crunchy crisps on the floor.
Snow!
Snow is layers of sugar.
Snow!
Snow is butter on a slice of bread.

Charlie Brough (10)
Marlborough Primary School

Snow

It's like a blank sheet of paper,
Coloured in with children playing,
When it disappears,
It's like the paper being torn up.

It's like a bed sheet settled on,
A big, green, muddy bed.
When it disappears,
It's like the sheets going in the wash.

It's like an explosion in a pillow factory,
All the feathers on the floor.
When it disappears,
It's like someone sweeping it up.

When you touch it, it's like powder.
It's cold, smooth and quiet.

You have joy inside you, you want to cry,
It's like a winter wonderland.

Olivia Megan Wheeldon (10)
Marlborough Primary School

The Snow

The snow comes down like feather dust,
It is as soft as cotton,

The snow is an egg without a yolk,
Comes down very quietly like water dripping.

Snow is paper across the ground ready to be coloured,
When you see it, there are tears of joy running down your face.

It smells fresh like perfume,
Snow is like a white bed sheet after it's washed.

Snow brings back nice memories,
When you see snow you feel happy and full of fun.

Snow is just soft snow.

Sofia Abdula (10)
Marlborough Primary School

Snow!

Sliding people on the floor,
Watching them get more and more.

Snow falling as white as a sheet,
Gazing at people with white feet.

Viewing the snow fall and fall,
Over the big, large, red walls.

Snow as thick as cream,
With a lovely sparkle and a beam.

Snow is just like icing on a cake,
Watching it bake and bake.

It is a beautiful white sheet,
Gleaming while it is very neat.

Seeing snow blow and blow,
In the winter while it flows.

Hodan Hassan (11)
Marlborough Primary School

Snow

Winter is as cold as a freezing cold fridge.
Snow is a creamy, fluffy sugar that people eat with strawberries.
When you stride on the snow it goes *crunch, crunch!*
Children like building snowmen and it creates joy.
When there is snow all over, it is like a spectacular world.

Hayley Louise Wood (10)
Marlborough Primary School

Snow

Snow
Snow is like icing on top of the earth.

Snow
Snow is a clear blanket of white.

Snow
Snow is like frozen stars falling from the sky.

Snow
Snow is the joy of Christmas.

Snow
Snow is the symbol of your dreams coming true.

Muhammad Mahmoud (11)
Marlborough Primary School

Snow

S now is an iced bun, all pretty and squishy.
N early everybody is having fun on the blank piece of paper.
O rchards have been covered with glitters and sparkles.
W inter snow is a sheet over a bumpy bed.

Lily Simone Cyphus (11)
Marlborough Primary School

What Is Snow?

Snow is white
But very bright.

It sparkles in the night
Twinkles very bright.

It crackles in the wind
It blows through my ear.

It feels so cold
But looks so smooth.

I like snow
But it's very cold
In the winter as it blows.

Snow is like frozen milk
Crunchy, munchy and so sweet.

Snow is white
But very bright.

When I see snow, I see joy
In the eyes of little boys.

Snow is icing on a cake
Watching while it bakes.

Snow is white
But very bright.

Tega Akpoduado (10)
Marlborough Primary School

Snow!

There's snow falling
It's lovely, nice and white.
It's as white and soft as cotton wool buds.
Snow is Antarctic rain.
Snowballs fall like bombs in war.
Snowmen are like snow-covered humans which attract humans
Who have never seen snow before.
Roll, roll as fast as you can, this has to be a big one
For the snowman!

Paul Hutchings (10)
Marlborough Primary School

Snow

Snow is fun!
Snow is bad!
Snow is fluffy and white!
Snow is cold in your hands!
Snow is falling from the sky!
Snow is fast and slow!
Snow is the most magnificent thing in the world!
Snow is cool!

Cameron Knights (11)
Marlborough Primary School

Snow!

Snow is a white sheet of paper that has been enlarged.
Snow is a thousand white coins that are as light as a feather which falls from the sky.
Snow is a blanket of whiteness and coldness which feels icy on your face.

People are rushing around like ants in an anthill.
Collisions in the town are hectic and chaotic.
The snow patters like tiny feet on an icy cold ground.
It is like a sprinkle of sugar on a happy day, it makes the day sweeter and lively until the snow melts.
It melts and melts and melts away into the darkness.
Nothing is left but ice and water.

Sahr Mian (11)
Marlborough Primary School

Snow

The snow is a pack of beautiful white blobs falling from the sky.
Snowmen are snow creatures.
Snowballs are bombs of snow.
Children running through the wet, soggy sludge.
Chaos on transport with roads, railways and runways closed.
Kicking footballs in the slush.
Snow, Third World War has broken out and people
 are shouting, 'Ouch!'
Get your gloves and hats on, we are ready for war!

Nathan-Lee Scotts (11)
Marlborough Primary School

The Snow

It looks like a glistening crystal.
Snowflakes are like metal raindrops.
The snow is cold as a freezer.
My fingers are cold as icicles.
Skiing is fun and very fast.
The snowballs are like cotton wool buds.
I love the snow!

Holly Dawkins-Hirst (11)
Marlborough Primary School

Let It Snow, Let It Snow, Let It Snow

A blanket of snow like a quilt of white cotton,
Warming up the car and frustrated parents,
More and more accidents on the M4 like World War Three
In the Arctic,
Lots of cold children like yoghurts in a freezer,
Can be a weapon of parts of the body, this is frostbite,
Snowflakes leaping through the air like snow leopards
In the mountains melting slowly.

James Hawes (11)
Marlborough Primary School

The Snow Is . . .

The snow is the Earth's seabed,
The snow is a layout on the ground,
The falling snow sprinkles like fairy dust from the sky,
The snow is as quiet as a library,
The snow is as crunchy as a chocolate bar.

Tayo Foluso-Henry (10)
Marlborough Primary School

Snow

Snow is the Earth's soft, fluffy, white blanket,
It is a glistening material, I wish I could thank it.

It is a big game that is fun for the family,
Even if it gets you wet, you still play happily.

It is white candyfloss with a sweetening taste,
It is like a joke that puts a smile on your face.

Snow fights and snowmen, lots to enjoy,
Forget about the texture, it is just like a toy.

Jodie O'Farrell (10)
Marlborough Primary School

Snow

Snow is the Earth's magical seabed waiting for snow to fall on it.
Snow is like a cold blanket stuffed with cotton wool.
Snow is like pink candyfloss that has been dyed white.
Snowballs are like white mints stuck together to make a snowball.

Snow is a cloud that has been dropped from Heaven.
Snow is like grey concrete painted white.
It's a colourful rug which has been dyed white.
Snow is a winter wonderland.

Snowmen's eyes are like dark chocolates.
Snow is like ice that has been frozen over the night sky.
Snow is a word that brings laughter and joy.
Snow is amazing and magical and when it falls it looks like
Glistening glitter.

Sabrina Singh (10)
Marlborough Primary School

Snow

Snow is Earth's mystical blanket,
Snow is a swarm of mythical silver insects,

Snow is the glacial breath of God,
Snow is the extraordinary gleaming White Sea,

Snow is the feather of a colossal dove,
Snow is what makes the charming moon shine,

Snow is a brass band of white angels,
Snow is the supreme rival or inferno flames,

Snow is the fiercest of all creatures,
Snow is the powerful emperor of cold.

Joshua Scurville (10)
Marlborough Primary School

Snow

Snow, snow, it's icy cold, penguins play in it too.
Making snowballs, having fun all the time.
The snow is cold, the snow is soft.
Snow is funny, snow is bad.
Snow is the best, you can never test.
Snow is the best.
Never gets hot when it snows, always cold.
Oh my God, it's snowing Mum!
Winter is very cold.

Ben Langham (10)
Marlborough Primary School

Snow

Snow is the world's hidden secret of fun
It is white fluffy candyfloss dropping out of the puffy clouds
It pours down like flickering dominoes onto the firm ground ready to settle
The delighted children jump and dance in the delicate layer
The icy road over-trodden by the skidding, rushing cars driven by the stressed late workers
The dangling icicles gradually melt as the sun peeps around the blocking cloud.

Rishi Sharma (11)
Marlborough Primary School

Snow

Snow is frost and ice
Children think it's really nice.

Ponds are frozen, puddles too
Snow is crunching under your shoes.

People wrap up warm with scarves and hats
Wearing coats, even the cats.

Snow is soft and crystal-like
But it's very hard to ride a bike.

When the snow turns into slush
Children build snowmen in a rush.

Emily-Rose Lucas (11)
Marlborough Primary School

Snow Today

Snow is a white fluffy layer over the Earth when it's winter.

I like it when the snowflake lands softly on my tongue.

When the snowflakes shatter across England,
It reminds me of white fairies falling from the misty sky.

The snow settles like a white sparkling carpet put down on grass.

And at the end, the snow melts like it is forming into a dead sea.

Rosey Hogan Life (10)
Marlborough Primary School

Snow

Snow falls as white flakes

Snow is a deadly weapon to us because it is disruptive
And can be dangerous

It is very cold and wet

People love snow because we live in England
And we don't see snow very often

It is lovely for winter animals like polar bears.

Ryan Holmes (11)
Marlborough Primary School

It's Snowing!

Snow is a white soft blanket to keep the Earth warm.

Parents get frustrated whilst warming up the car.

Children as cheerful as babies with their rattles, building snowmen
And having fights.

On the radio, parents hear, 'Traffic on the M4',
And 'Traffic on the A6.'

Snow falling like small tears coming from the sky.

Back gardens full of children hurling snowballs at each other.

Finally the sun comes out as fierce as a lion
And slowly it all melts away.

Sabrina Sahota (10)
Marlborough Primary School

Winter's Miracles

The snow powers down like God is winning a battle
It's as white as a blank sheet of paper
The parks are wrapped up with its cold white blanket
The first breeze of snow lightens the day
Cars slip and slide like ice skating on wheels
Accidents happen because of the icy coating
Restricting vehicles, stopping and starting
Snow is like a white breezy sea
Snow sparkles as the flakes silently blow down
The white miracle is like the white fur upon a polar bear.

Jessica Bennett (10)
Marlborough Primary School

Snow Is Falling

Snow is falling
A beautiful sight,
Snow is falling
With the crispiest bite,
Snow is falling
It plays its game,
Snow is falling
It makes everything the same.
Snow is falling
The weather's dull and grey,
Snow is falling
The children pray for it to stay,
Snow is falling
It blinds all who see,
Snow is falling
It hides you from me,
From a cloud that is deep, high in the sky,
Snow is falling
In front of my glancing eye.

Maham Ijaz (11)
Marlborough Primary School

Silence

Silence tastes sour, like butterflies in your stomach.
Silence sounds like darkness, drifting through the air.
Silence looks like a room, clean and full of emptiness.
Silence reminds me of a small child, left all alone.
Silence is white, like a pure brand new sheet.
Silence is like an illness; it spreads and spreads, until they find
                                    the only cure of conversation.
Silence is a piece of paper, with not a single word.

Silence tastes unbearable, as sharp as a knife.
Silence sounds like a window, without a single view.
Silence looks like the wind, although you cannot see it,
                                    it's definitely there.
Silence reminds me of a fresh spring day, awaiting its very first flower.
Silence is black, like a huge gaping hole, just waiting for you to fall in.
Silence feels cold, like ice on a warm day.
Silence is like a classroom, where there's seldom any children.
Silence is a beautiful poem that's hidden in a book.

Emma Jade Flint (11)
Our Lady of Peace RC Junior School

Love

Love sounds like birds singing in the beautiful fresh air.
It smells like lying in a big field of rose-scented flowers.
Love reminds me of opening the door and finding hard
caramel sweets and a sweet smell of a Valentine's card.
It feels like fluttering butterflies in my tummy.
Love looks like a waterfall with flowers and sparkling hearts
coming down from the beautiful shiny water.
It tastes like a hot melted honey chocolate muffin slowly coming
into my dribbling mouth.

Kayleigh Irwin (10)
Our Lady of Peace RC Junior School

Love

Love is pink like your heart booming in your body.
It feels like a tingle in your body.
It sounds like two people dancing.
It reminds me of my dance.
It tastes like strawberry because it is so sweet.
It smells like perfumes mixed to smell nice.
It feels like a rose in my hand.
It smells like a bunch of roses.

Ben Buckley (10)
Our Lady of Peace RC Junior School

Silence

Silence is like a dark spooky night
when you can't even hear the mice
running around trying to find food.
Silence is like a group of nosy children
looking around an abandoned house
looking for things to do.

Silence is like friendship
one word can make all the difference.
Silence can be locked deep inside you
then all at once you can let it out unprecedented.

Silence is there when a funeral is on
because everyone is too sad to make a noise.
Silence is not there when there is a party on
because everyone is having too much fun
and does not care whether they make to much noise.

Silence can be anywhere.

Heidi Lansley (11)
Our Lady of Peace RC Junior School

Love

Love is like fireworks coming from the background.
Love feels like I am touching something soft.
Love smells like perfume that has just been sprayed.
Love looks like two people dancing in the moonlight.
Love sounds like two birds singing happily on a quiet day.
Love tastes like cherries on top of a cheesecake.
Love reminds me of my mum and dad's first date.

Georgina Irwin (10)
Our Lady of Peace RC Junior School

Anger

Anger is red like a fierce wild fire.
Anger feels like getting cut in the throat with a razor-sharp knife.
Anger sounds like a young child screaming.
Anger looks like the eye of a furious raging bull.
Anger smells like black smoke from a blazing fire.
Anger tastes like a big sour sweet bursting in your mouth.
Anger reminds me of my mum having chocolates
                                   and not letting me have any.
Anger is red like blood dripping from a dead body.
Anger feels like being ripped apart by a great white shark.
Anger sounds like the Devil chuckling non-stop.
Anger looks like a fierce exploding volcano.
Anger smells like lava burning a small village.
Anger tastes like a burning piece of chilli on my tongue.
Anger reminds me of falling in a blazing hot volcano.

Adam Orr (10)
Our Lady of Peace RC Junior School

Happiness

Happiness is pink
Just like a laughing baby.

Happiness tastes like candyfloss
Melting in your mouth.

Happiness reminds me of my black cat
Purring against my leg.

Happiness smells like your favourite popcorn
Bursting out of the microwave.

Happiness looks like a yellow field
Covered with grinning flowers.

Happiness feels like a child
Jumping on your back, giggling with glee.

Cristina Lucci (10)
Our Lady of Peace RC Junior School

Fear

Fear smells like black raging smoke that makes you feel sick.
Fear reminds me of a red devil that comes and jumps on my back.
It looks like a red dragon swooping over my head.
Fear is a thousand dead corpses.
Fear tastes like burnt ashes swimming around in my mouth.

Joseph Allen (11)
Our Lady of Peace RC Junior School

Fear

I see something dark and fearful that lies ahead of me
under the fear and darkness.
For now I will forget it but in the future I'll meet it
and could possibly die.
I have not met my fear yet so I know it will come.
Maybe in a day, maybe in a year, my heart tells me it's a great fear
because some people have got theirs or found theirs.
Fear looks like a pitch-black room.
It feels like a room with evil inside.
Fear smells like coal in a barbecue fire burning and breaking.
Fear reminds me of something dreadful and horrifying.
If I meet it I will fight, if I don't I won't.

Rajiv Vadher (10)
Our Lady of Peace RC Junior School

Silence

Silence is white like a cloud drifting away in the blue sky.
It looks like a massive crowd with no mouths but just hands.
Silence feels like a blank piece of white paper.
It smells like an empty cinema after a movie.
Silence sounds like a graveyard in the morning.
It can be broken with one small word.

Silence can be fun, it depends what you're doing.
Silence can be bad, it depends what you're doing.
It sounds like the ocean hitting the beach.
It can happen anytime, anywhere.
Silence feels like a white soft cloud.
It can be broken with one small word.

Matt Mault (11)
Our Lady of Peace RC Junior School

Loneliness

Loneliness feels like being lonely in the dark blue sea.
Loneliness reminds me of having no friends and being invisible.
Loneliness smells like a new piece of paper.
Loneliness looks like being in jail with no one to comfort you.

Parondeep Sandhu (10)
Our Lady of Peace RC Junior School

Life

Life is like a board game,
You take chances with a dice,
When you're feeling happy,
You move up a space,
When you're feeling sad,
You go back to the start.

Life is like a board game,
You need a friend,
Just like you need one to play the game,
Sometimes you win,
Sometimes you lose.

Life is sometimes a sweet fruity scent,
But is sometimes old and damp,
It is sometimes bright and sunny
And sometimes dark and scary.

Life is like a board game,
You need a helping hand,
You need to learn the rules of the game,
It reminds me of snakes and ladders,
A game I love to play.

Life is like a board game.
Life,
Life,
Life.

Christie Jeffries (11)
Our Lady of Peace RC Junior School

The Sky

The sky looks amazing and bright, it's also blue and white.
You see the spectacular birds flying in the sky,
just like you want to join them to fly.
You hear the sounds of the robins whistling,
soaring through the trees.
The sky carries the sun, when it comes out you have a lot of fun.
At night-time you look at the sky with the stars sparkling.
The bright blue and white sky reminds you of a nice hot holiday.
The sky smells like lovely fresh air.
The sky is wonderful.
Everyone loves the sky, why? I just don't know.
The sky is beautiful.

Rohan Wattley (11)
Our Lady of Peace RC Junior School

Happiness

Happiness is a wonderful thing
It makes us glow warm inside
Having fun brings us happiness
Happiness can make you laugh with joy.

Happiness feels like skipping through a park
It makes us feel happy inside
Happiness feels like doing something for the first time
Being happy is fun and great.

It sounds like children giggling and laughing
Happiness is like making a new friend
Happiness sounds like getting something you always wanted
Happiness sounds like a monkey's laugh echoing through the jungle.

Happiness looks like grinning flowers in the sun
It is like a new, fresh, golden meadow
Happiness looks like Heaven in the clouds
It is like playing on a sunny beach.

It tastes like eating candyfloss
It tastes like eating popcorn for the first time
It's like the smell of freshly made cakes
It smells like flowers.

Happiness is yellow like a lovely sunny day
It reminds me of two best friends forever
It's like two best friends talking together
Happiness is a wonderful thing.

Beth Quarterman (10)
Our Lady of Peace RC Junior School

Happiness Is Like . . .

Happiness reminds me of a flower in an empty field with no one in it.
Happiness smells like candyfloss in your mouth.
Happiness feels like a friendship with everyone in it.
Happiness looks like the best flower in the summer.
Happiness tastes like eating sweets for the first time.
Happiness sounds like lots of people having fun.
Happiness is pink like a baby when it is born.

Happiness reminds me of a white snowball in the air.
Happiness smells like a new flower with all its leaves.
Happiness feels like having fun.
Happiness looks like a new friendship that will never end.
Happiness tastes like water running round your mouth.
Happiness sounds like laughter exploding into your ears.
Happiness is yellow, it lights up every room if it needs lighting up.
Happiness is only a second away.

Alex Shaw (10)
Our Lady of Peace RC Junior School

Love

Love looks like a great huge heart.
It tastes like love potion gushing out.
Love feels like a friend who is loving and loyal.
It reminds me of the summer with flowers all around.
Love smells like fresh air rushing through your system.
It sounds like a heart beating constantly.

Love looks like a smiley face.
It tastes like boxes of chocolates.
Love feels like a big cuddly bear ready to hug you.
It reminds me of butterflies flying around.
Love smells like the gorgeous smell of perfume.
It sounds like birds singing in the trees.

Love looks like a waterfall powering out love.
It tastes like sweet tropical fruit.
Love feels like friends being reunited.
It reminds me of Valentine's Day.
Love smells like strawberries and cream.
It sounds like people laughing with joy.

Mary Porter (11)
Our Lady of Peace RC Junior School

Hunger

Hunger is the colour black
because when you see it you want to turn back.

Hunger smells like rotten fish
because you can't put it on a meal or dish.

Hunger reminds me of forgtting my lunch
or someone stealing and getting a punch.

Hunger looks like a very sick goat
because there is nothing to cleanse his throat.

Hunger feels like you're on fire inside
you can run but there's nowhere to hide.

Charlie Thomas (10)
Our Lady of Peace RC Junior School

Light

Light is white, bright and shiny.
It looks like a white creature creeping inside a room.
It feels like a sparkling light is entering my body.
Its sound is nothingness, plain as day.
Light is a path, it is the right way.
Light tastes like gleaming stars impaling me.
    Light is infinity.

Luke Thomas (11)
Our Lady of Peace RC Junior School

Chocolate Bar

Let me tell you about my smooth creamy friend.
She's always sweet to the very, very end.
It accompanies me when I'm hungry to fill up the hole.
I run my fingers down the side of the smooth oblong shape.
When I can't resist it anymore I break a chunk and it goes crack.
The peppermint fragrance wafts past my nose, fills the air
like a sweet-smelling rose.
When I can't resist it anymore, I break a chunk and in it goes.
What am I?
Well my friend of course is an amazing chocolate bar.
Ha, ha, ha.

Samara Richardson (11)
Our Lady of Peace RC Junior School

Darkness

Darkness is black,
It's like the pupil in your eye.

Darkness is the sound of somebody screaming,
Like the wind blowing in the trees.

Darkness smells of the fear,
Darkness smells like a mistake.

Darkness looks like a dreadful forest.

Darkness feels like an eye, all slimy,
Nothing else to touch.

Patrick Smyth (10)
Our Lady of Peace RC Junior School

Silence

Silence is white, a whisper in the elegant winds.
It sounds like nothing used by peaceful actions.
It feels like a breeze of new beginnings that drift past your mind.
Silence looks like a clean white blanket over those in gentle minds.
It tastes like a breath of fresh air filling each heart with wonder.
Silence smells like a newborn rose risen from its bud.
It reminds me of a black wonder, which everyone follows in peace
                                                              and will forever.

Sophie Holder (11)
Our Lady of Peace RC Junior School

Lightning

Lightning is a zigzag of electricity,
an explosion of high voltage.
It crashes through the cities and silences the villages.
While parents sleep, children weep,
while children weep, their parents keep.
Everyone is silent when the terrible noise smashes through.
Lightning is God's loudest cymbals, louder than a sonic boom,
never, never fading away.

Toby Whatley (10)
Our Lady of Peace RC Junior School

Silence

Silence is white, an empty room.
Silence is black, a dark empty room.
It doesn't make any noise . . . silence,
It's a huge silence.
It tastes like hollow air,
The aroma is like a free place.
It looks like a man with a closed mouth sitting like a child
In the corner in the darkness.
It feels like bursting out into laughter.
It feels sorrowful.

Dominika Kwiatkowska (10)
Our Lady of Peace RC Junior School

Guess Who?

If you melt me I will be tasteless
but if you have just come from a scorching hot desert
I will be very, very refreshing and enjoyable.

What am I?

Daniel Crouch (10)
Our Lady of Peace RC Junior School

Apple Crumble

When I wake upon a warm summer's day
And my tummy starts to rumble,
I have this urge to eat a plate of apple crumble.
Sugar, ice cream and maybe a blob of custard,
But don't you dare try it with baking hot mustard.
When midday comes and the cupboards are bare,
I want some apple crumble not orange or pear.
Sugar, ice cream and maybe a blob of custard,
But don't you dare try it with boiling hot mustard.

Stefano Duarte Gouveia (11)
Our Lady of Peace RC Junior School

Smoker Stinker

The tar-filled smell of the smoking twigs,
The smokers smell of dirty big pigs.
They sound like sick people wheezing away,
But before they know it they'll be dying one day.
They look like beggars with no money to spare,
But carry on without a single care.
It seems to me they're not going to stop,
If they don't they're in for the chop.
They smoke, smoke, smoke all life long,
Has anyone told them they're in the wrong?
To me smoking is a coughing hell
And that's not including the horrendous smell.
So take my advice they're going to die soon,
If you start smoking you're an absolute loon!

Oliver Hodge (10)
Our Lady of Peace RC Junior School

Giraffes

Giraffes are silky, some places rough,
When running at speed they're very tough.
Clattering forward like an elegant deer,
With big ears to hear if you are near.
Related to horses some people may say,
They eat thorns and also hay.
Tall and spotted like leopards they look,
If you want to know more read an animal book.

Fiona Hughes (11)
Our Lady of Peace RC Junior School

Laughter

Laughter is multicoloured, it's lots of things put together.
It sounds like a theme park, children screaming.
It sounds like a baby crying until it has no voice.
It feels like a bubble about to burst.
It looks like a person that's just been hurt.
It smells like little children that have been cursed.
It tastes like flavoured water bobbing up
and down in my stomach making me laugh.

Daniela Ioviero (10)
Our Lady of Peace RC Junior School

The Ladybird

Fluttering and twittering in the sky
She's quietly creeping among the plants
Landing on flower after flower in the gardens nearby
She doesn't make a sound, she is as quiet as can be
She looks like a petite little spot buzzing when she flies
We have probably all seen her
You and me.

Alice Kearley (11)
Our Lady of Peace RC Junior School

Hunger

Hunger is red in your body.
It sounds like the water boiling in a hot, scorching kettle.
It looks like a squashed banana which is lying on the road.
The aroma is like a muffin across the street coming from the baker's.
It feels like a dry, sore throat which makes you cough.
It also feels like gigantic bubbles playing with your tummy.

Waqar Shafi (11)
Our Lady of Peace RC Junior School

A Magic Pencil

I've got a pink pencil in my pocket
which talks to me at night.
It doesn't like to be in silence
and see the sunshine bright.
Sometimes it flies far away from me
but I don't care about it,
it comes back quickly.
I don't really want it to be with me
but this pencil likes me, as you can see.
Pencil, oh pencil, what shall I do?
Pencil, oh pencil, you know it's you,
that keeps me awake at a quarter to two.
Sleeping in the day, talking at night
and can't even see the sunshine bright.

Dominika Krawczyk (10)
Our Lady of Peace RC Junior School

Sweets, Glorious Sweets

I love my sweets
because they are much more delicious than meat.
Refreshers and gobstoppers are a treat
and definitely Smarties can't be beat
and they certainly don't come better than lollipops.
But it's a draw between Haribos and Gummy Bops
but I guess it all comes to me being chubby
like a cat which is extremely tubby.

Oscar Ness (10)
Our Lady of Peace RC Junior School

Darkness

Staring into darkness all alone
Wolves whistling, owls tooting
Freezing and damp as it starts to hail
Salty sea is in your mouth
Wolves whistling, owls tooting
In the blackness of the night.

Bethany Worth (11)
Our Lady of Peace RC Junior School

Fire

Fire with glistening flames and dancing waves of light.
Fire with noises like a golden pen clicking as the button
                                                is pushed down hard.
Fire can sound like a lost child crying for his mother.
Fire feels like an explosion of burning blisters.
Fire tastes like someone is ruthlessly whipping your gut.
Fire smells like a car starting as it emits musty black smoke.
Fire looks like a luring and glamorous colourful light.

Luke Connor (11)
Our Lady of Peace RC Junior School

Darkness

Darkness feels like a crocodile's skin.
It looks like a nightmare that will never end.
Darkness smells like thick black smoke coming out of a fire.
Darkness sounds like fingernails scraping down the walls.
It tastes like rotting bones.

Ryan Stevens
Our Lady of Peace RC Junior School

Anger

Anger feels like I . . . I . . . I just want to blow up like an atomic bomb.
It looks like a never-ending snowy mountain you just have to climb.
Anger smells like the burning of an ever-lasting bonfire.
It sounds like fingernails scraping down a blackboard.
Anger tastes like sewer water flowing through 100-year-old tunnels.

Connor Swan (10)
Our Lady of Peace RC Junior School

Anger Poem

Anger feels like a wrinkly old face.
Anger feels like a rough shoelace.
Anger smells like smoke building up
Always flowing up to the top.
Anger looks like an ugly old man
Eyes red-hot like a frying pan.
Anger tastes like a mouldy hen
It often comes now and again.
Anger sounds like an evil spirit
If you live life you have to live with it.

Jake Wheatley (10)
Our Lady of Peace RC Junior School

Anger

Anger feels like sharp teeth going through your body.
It feels like a mountain throwing out fire.
Anger looks like a body throwing blood at other people
turning into monsters.
Anger looks like standing over a dead body.
Anger looks like a dead man standing.

Rochelle John (10)
Our Lady of Peace RC Junior School

Pride

Pride tastes like victory over your nearest rivals.
Pride smells like the sweet sensation of flowers.
Pride feels like when you first ride a bike.
Pride looks like a man with nothing in his way.
Pride sounds like you're walking through a garden of flowers.

Jack January (10)
Our Lady of Peace RC Junior School

Sadness

Sadness feels like the earth giving way underneath your feet,
Like you're being sucked into a black hole.

It looks like a never-ending hall of darkness,
Like being surrounded by the Devil and his horrifying minions
Laughing at you.

Sadness smells like the dingiest sewer
Surrounding you with its poisonous stench.

It tastes like the bitterness of mouldy lemons and rotting flesh.

Sadness sounds like the throbbing of a killer brain,
Like the beating of a surviving heart trying to find its body.

Sadness makes me want to fly away,
To hide away in my own imaginary world
And leave it all behind.

Aaron Wetton (11)
Our Lady of Peace RC Junior School

Nervous

Nervous looks like a never-ending black path to victory,
While goblins are shaking the floor underneath you
And you've never noticed.

If feels like an earthquake from beneath your feet,
Putting your hands in an electric box and getting electrocuted.

Nervous sounds like a scream with 300 amps echoing in a tunnel,
It's bursting your eardrum.

Nervous tastes like a full English breakfast,
But suddenly it burns and you just want to throw it up.

It smells like fire in Hell,
Praying to get to Heaven.

Nervous is like World War II,
It's filling my head with nightmares.

Jack Tucker (10)
Our Lady of Peace RC Junior School

Fun

Fun looks like rainbows and the sun in the sky shining over everybody.
Fun sounds like children playing and kids laughing.
Fun smells like melted chocolate bubbling away and smells like walking into a sweet shop.
Fun tastes like candyfloss tickling the back of my throat.
Fun feels like fluffy marshmallows because if you fall you will bounce back and your fun will never get ruined.

Roisín Molloy (11)
Our Lady of Peace RC Junior School

Losing

Losing sounds like the world is mocking you.
Losing tastes like victory gone sour.
Losing feels like having something you almost had wrenched
                                                         out of your grasp.
Losing smells like rotting food.
Losing looks like rain on your wedding day.

Rhiannon Wood (11)
Our Lady of Peace RC Junior School

Love Poem

Love feels like a fluffy cloud.
Love looks like a golden angel.
Love smells like something so beautiful I can't describe it.
Love sounds like angels singing.
Love tastes like chocolate.
Love makes me feel happy and joyful.

Laura Gotts (10)
Our Lady of Peace RC Junior School

Jumping For Joy

Joy feels soft like a fluffy cushion.
It looks like a dandelion gleaming in the sun.
Joy smells like a petal of a rose.
Joy sounds like a wave crashing.
It tastes like a perfect pancake.
Joy makes me want to scream with happiness.

Sam Wealleans (10)
Our Lady of Peace RC Junior School

Hate

It feels like a stingray's tail has pierced through my heart.
It tastes like green mouldy sandwiches that have been
in my smelly PE bag for a year,
the fungi is eating away at my liver.
It's a scorching bacterial stench that's getting to me,
it's making me frustrated.
It sounds like a tsunami jumping over houses
and knocking them over.
It looks like a raging fight just about to erupt.

Patrick Bart (10)
Our Lady of Peace RC Junior School

Love

Love feels soft like a feather.
Love looks like a big fluffy cloud from Heaven sent to Earth.
Love smells like a scented candle lighting,
filling the room with fragrance all day and night.
Love sounds like a nice calm music when you're down or happy.
Love tastes like something I can't describe
but I know it's something nice and beautiful.

Chloe Park (10)
Our Lady of Peace RC Junior School

Anger

Anger is sharp like a dragon's tooth.
Anger looks like a wall of pain.
Anger smells like drops of blood falling from a tiger's mouth.
Anger sounds like a man being killed.
Anger tastes like stale blood.
Anger is like a never-ending wall of pain.

Jamie Crouch (10)
Our Lady of Peace RC Junior School

Love Poem

Love feels like a gigantic fluffy cloud.
Love looks like a glittering golden angel.
Love smells like something so delicious I cannot possibly describe it.
Love tastes like juicy red strawberries pouring with juice.
Love sounds like angels singing quietly.

Charlie Watkins (11)
Our Lady of Peace RC Junior School

Fear

Fear sounds like the Devil screaming
A piercing tune as if you're dreaming.
When fear chases you down a winding path
All your enemies look at you and they just laugh.
Fear's behind you on a bike,
It smells of things you've never liked.
Fear feels like a hard ball,
But when you've overcome it, it feels so small.
Your life turns into a flexible path
And it moves up just like a graph.
Fear can sometimes give you the scare,
But when you overcome it you'll feel like the town mayor.

Liam Bibby (11)
Our Lady of Peace RC Junior School

Laughter

Laughter looks like lovely, kind, wild animals
and plants all around me.
It feels like a marshmallow or a massive trampoline
that I can fall back on.
Laughter smells like freshly baked cookies just out the oven.
It sounds like birds singing happily in the sunshine.
It tastes like strawberries with cream.

Emma Johnston (11)
Our Lady of Peace RC Junior School

Anger

Anger feels like a knife piercing my heart.
Anger looks like a waterfall that I have to go down.
Anger smells like something I can't describe.
Anger sounds like a bomb exploding in my hand.
Anger tastes like a pig that has been rolling around in soggy mud.

George Clark (10)
Our Lady of Peace RC Junior School

Sadness

Sadness feels like the river isn't flowing,
It feels like the rain is pouring and it isn't going to end.
It looks like the sea of tears you have to swim.
Sadness smells like mouldy milk, it makes people faint.
Sadness sounds like a child that has broken their leg.
Sadness looks like mouldy hearts with liver and eggs
with mustard smothered on it.

Sophie Boyce (10)
Our Lady of Peace RC Junior School

Love Poem

Love feels like swaying side to side on a cloud of love.
Love looks like a layered wedding cake, layer after layer
of perfect rich food ingredients for a beautiful couple.
Love smells like organic scents in an aromatherapy kit.
Love tastes like an organic smoothie with beautiful vanilla ice cream.
Love sounds like calming music with a lullaby sung caringly
to a baby by their mother.

Sidonie Satchell (10)
Our Lady of Peace RC Junior School

Cigarettes

Cigarettes taste like a burning stick
They feel like pieces of paper
When you light them they flicker
They smell like a big fire
With a big electric wire
Big cigarettes look like a burning tree
Cigarettes descend very quickly.

Kamran Atwal (10)
Our Lady of Peace RC Junior School

Poor Little Monkey

How poor is he,
Not in a tree,
All his life,
Without a wife,
The little monkey in a cage.

What has he done
To deserve no fun?
His fur in rags,
The time slowly drags,
Sad little monkey in a cage.

No branches here,
He lives in fear,
The noise of cars,
His dull grey bars,
Poor little monkey in a cage.

Sebastian Huddy (11)
Our Lady's Preparatory School

The Aliens

The aliens are coming
Down to planet Earth
And the people are running,
Wondering what to do,
The aliens are coming and they're gonna get you.

The Earth is in peril,
They don't have a clue,
Even MI5 don't know what to do.

People are being abducted
And tested on a spaceship,
The aliens are using weapons
Stranger than can be
As the people are being incinerated
By the aliens from planet Mercury.

Ben Cross (11)
Our Lady's Preparatory School

Fire Kennings

Brick melter
Coal burner

Smoke maker
Water hater

Air breather
Fire eater

Animal hater
Plant killer

Wood muncher
Sand dodger

House burner
Big spreader

Heat seeker
Forest killer

Good heater
Marshmallow melter.

Miguel O'Donnell (10)
Our Lady's Preparatory School

Hunt, Chase, Capture

Hiding in the undergrowth
The rabbits cannot see me,
Bushy tail behind a tree,
Soon to pounce when they are close,
My hungry cubs need a meal
That is why I have to steal.

With a rabbit in my mouth,
Going to hide in my den,
They can never find me then.
They may be chasing me now
But the hunters do not know,
All the places I can go.

In the place where my cubs hide
How could they have found me here?
How could they have got so near?
I see them getting closer,
I have to protect my young,
I don't want to, but I'll run.

Robin Fenlon (10)
Our Lady's Preparatory School

The Tiger In The Zoo

I love to go and see the tiger
Who lives in London Zoo.
He lives right next door to the penguins,
I also like them too.

He snarls and growls at everyone
Who happens to walk by.
Once I saw him growl so loud
He made a little boy cry.

His name is Tommy
But I call him Tom.
He's moved away now,
I'm so sad that he has gone.

Chantelle Brennan (11)
Our Lady's Preparatory School

Sun

The sun is a big orange ball high in the sky
that glows with fire and energy.
Twelve hours on half the planet and twelve on the other
bringing light to all the world.

The sun shines on the crops
turning them to a golden brown
and helping them to grow.
We need it for warmth and heat
and bright shining light.

All around light shines on me,
I feel happy and bright.

Luke Bainbridge (10)
Our Lady's Preparatory School

London Zoo

I can see a lion roaring in its cage.
I can see a mother letting out her rage.

I can see a gorilla beating on its chest,
I can see a bird in a tree making its cosy nest.

I can see a snake slithering away,
I can see children coming in for the day.

I can see the zebras running in the field,
I can see a little girl eating her meal.

I can see the giraffes waiting for their food,
I can see people having fun at London Zoo.

Sammie Liu (10)
Our Lady's Preparatory School

Red Is For Danger

Red is for danger
If you see red
Then you should stop
Or there will be nasty accident.

If you see a person
Lying on the floor
You should stop quickly
And see if they are poorly.

If you don't stop
At the red light
You may end up in hospital
With a broken arm and leg.

If you do not wait at a red light
You will be risking your life
And other's too
Red is for danger.

Matthew Prior (10)
Our Lady's Preparatory School

The Blitz

The bombs come down
On London town,
Oh what a sight to see,
The sirens groan,
The children moan,
London is far from glee.

The fires are burning,
The families are churning,
Rubble builds very quickly,
The destruction is nigh,
We're all going to die,
Yes the bombs are destructive you see.

Reuben O'Brien (11)
Our Lady's Preparatory School

What Am I?

Tree swooper
           Fast mover
Long hanging
           Loud banging
Fruit eating
           Light sleeping
Cheeky face
           Around the place
Swinging around
           Upside down
Not too chunky
           I'm a monkey.

Simran Birring (11)
Radstock Primary School

It's A . . .

Scary jaws
Sharp claws
Amazing horns
Scales like thorns
Horny tail
Green scale
Human taker
Danger maker
Mythical creature
Has a lot of features
Breathes fire
Burns tyres

It's a . . . dragon.

Ammar Mohamed (11)
Radstock Primary School

It's A . . .

Sharp claws
Podgy paws
Very playful
Not at all tasteful
Nut eater
Light sleeper
Drink slurper
Nosy lurker
Loud squeaker
Bad leaper
Round ball of fluff
Nibbles at most stuff
Cute pet
Hates the vet
Not very big
I'm a . . . ?

Sarah Taylor (10)
Radstock Primary School

What Am I?

I'm a meat eater,
Loud greeter,
Creep around,
Not making a sound,
Fast terror,
Kitten scarer,
Muddy paws
Mum's hated chore,
I'm a really lucky
Small . . . *puppy.*

Anastasia Baker (10)
Radstock Primary School

It's A . . .

Sky slayer
Food player

Low swooper
Loop the looper

Meat eater
Carnivorous seeker

Speedy glider
Wind rider

Fast mover
Rabbit hoover

It's a *falcon!*

Zack Baddeley (11)
Radstock Primary School

What Am I?

Long tongue
Smelly dung

Likes bugs
Hates hugs

Rough skin
He blends in

Big eyes
That's a surprise

Changes colour
Never duller

A funny comedian
He's a . . .

Daniel Peacock (11)
Radstock Primary School

It's A . . .

Furry pillow
Near that willow
Long ears
Coming near
Ball of fluff
Very tough
Grass eater
Not a weeper
Hopping here
Having a cheer
Carrot lover
Under cover
In a hutch
Love her very much

It's a *rabbit.*

Kate Phillips (11)
Radstock Primary School

What Am I . . . ?

Meat eater
Heavy sleeper
Ball of fluff
Very tough
Long pouncer
High bouncer
Fierce creature
Cool feature
Big jaws
Small claws

I am a . . . ?

Wolf.

Nico Vazquez-Oliveira (10)
Radstock Primary School

Skunk To Skunk - Tanka

You smell like roses
From your head all the way down
You'll be mine some day.

You're a skunk which smells badly
You do not know what I'm like!

Gemma Kinch (11)
Radstock Primary School

I Love Dolphins!

Dolphins are extremely playful
They leap and splash all day
When it's time to feed on fish
No dolphin can delay.

>Dolphins are truly graceful
>Their bodies shine and gleam
>They'll sparkle in the sunshine
>And even in the moonbeams.

Dolphins are remarkably active
They all spend time being speedy
Even in lunchtimes they have to be quick
Though it doesn't prevent them from being greedy.

>Dolphins are very sociable
>They talk in whistles, squeaks and clicks
>When they're not chatting with friends
>They're busy playing tricks.

Dolphins are specially friendly
They'd never harm a flea
They're only greedy while eating fish
For breakfast, lunch or tea.

>I love dolphins a lot
>They're so sweet and clever
>They are my favourite animal
>I'll never forget them, ever.

Sakshi Raizada (10)
Wessex Primary School

My Best Mate And Me!

We both like the colour pink,
We enjoy skating on an ice rink.
We play together and have lots of fun,
Our favourite weather is the sun.
One of our hobbies is to sing together,
We'll be best mates forever.

One day we'll grow up to be adults,
I hope that when we're older we'll get good results.
We like eating chips,
We hate parsnips.
We'll go through good and bad things together,
We'll be best mates forever.

We sing and dance together,
We hope to do this forever and ever.
We wish to be friends for years and years,
We'll go through laughter and tears,
Will we ever argue? Never,
We'll be best mates forever.

Leah Collins (10)
Wessex Primary School

Life

Superheroes, the movies, shapes and the zoo,
Months, seasons, aliens too.
Plants, gardens, holidays and foods,
Humans, fairies, people with moods.

Rulers, pencils, marbles and paper,
If you have got a bad back you can use vapour.
Stereos, CDs, aerials and buttons,
Maybe a tabby cat called Muttons.

Mothers, brothers, sisters, misters,
Maybe no socks (lots of blisters!)
Crunch, munch, maybe no lunch.

Maybe the Olympics,
Or a bag of pick and mix,
Spending money
Fluffy bunny.

That's my life!

Grace Perfect (9)
Wessex Primary School

Let's Party!

Time for partying
Get all the food
Cake and biscuits
Helps you get in the mood!

Get down and boogie
Do some dancing
Shake all over
And get that bum movin'.

Boys try dancing
But the girls will show them how
Everybody's dancing
Just listen to the music, *wow!*

Everybody has arrived
Wear some party hats
Lots and lots of presents
And lay down the party mats.

Everybody's as happy
As a cheeky monkey
People are eating so much
Their bellies are getting chunky.

Hang up the decorations
The drinks have come
Oh my favourite
A little bit of rum.

Having a party involves balloons
Everybody's wearing different clothes
Even Britney came
Doing her pose.

Katie Hawkins (9)
Wessex Primary School

My Art Teacher

I have an art teacher,
Mrs Hillborne is her name.
She's a real golden girl
And art is her game.

She's supergirl,
Expert with paint and paper.
She's a multicoloured diva
With her ball of fab ideas.

She has flashy, flashy fashion,
She's purple, pink, red, white and black,
She's 100% an artist.

I like her lots,
She's a tip-top arty,
                    arty,
                            arty,
                                  arty
                                      queen.

Daisy Fox (9)
Wessex Primary School

Fairy Tales

I love fairy tales
They're so magical
Lots of exciting characters
Everything's fantastical
Rapunzel grows her hair long
Sleeping Beauty sleeps
Cinderella can't go to the ball
So she sits and weeps
Snow White met the dwarfs
She cleans their house all day
When the dwarfs come home
Dopey wants to play
Robin Hood is great
He defeats the bad
He comes to save the poor people
He's a super lad
That's why I love fairy tales
They make me well when I'm not
I have a thick fairy tale book
And in it there's an awful lot.

Leyan Yucel (10)
Wessex Primary School

Fairies!

Most people don't have experience with fairies like I do,
They're as beautiful as the rising sun,
When they marry they say, 'I do!'

> A long time ago,
> There were two fairies,
> That decided to marry each other,
> Soon enough the young woman chose to become a mother.

Fairies are much more beautiful,
Than you see in books,
But I'm afraid you can't compare,
With any of their good looks.

> Very caring and generous,
> You'll never be alone,
> Precious and extremely valuable,
> Like a beautiful stone.

Fairies are very special things,
Would you like to know why?
Shall I tell you? Yes I will
I'm amazed they can fly.

> Sometimes fairies tickle your feet
> When you're asleep in bed,
> They make you feel much cosier,
> They create an image in your head.

Fairies are so magical,
They can cast spells for good,
Weather fairies, party fairies, rainbow fairies, the lot,
They act like Robin Hood.

Jennifer Barnard (9)
Wessex Primary School

I'm Going To The Zoo

I'm going to the zoo
On a Sunday afternoon
I can't wait to get there
I wonder if I'll see a bear.

I was amazed to see
A chimpanzee
I love to see the seals
Eating their meals.

I feel sorry for the animals in their cages
They must have been in there for ages
When I'm older I want to be a zookeeper
I wonder if I'll have to wear a beeper.

Once on a school trip I went to Whipsnade Zoo
It was very fun there I met someone called Sue.

Megan Robson (10)
Wessex Primary School

Valuable Things

Some valuable things
Are not worth much money,
Whether it's a teddy bear
Or a toy bunny.

Poor people don't
Have much food
They don't have many valuable things
That is why they're not always in a good mood.

Some poor children
Have never had
Anything like
A mum or dad.

To buy a diamond
You need lots of money to spend
But nothing is more valuable than
A family and a friend.

Alicia Carrington (9)
Wessex Primary School

Butterflies

A butterfly flying in the air
Is such a pretty sight
I can see a pair soaring
With all of their might.

Now they are in the sky
Showing their colour out
Along the way they cry
I am ready to fly.

They fly past birds
And aeroplanes
Saying words
While it rains.

Now they have reached their journey's end
Reaching their destination
Meeting their friends again
And that's all part of their creation.

Louise Cockrell (9)
Wessex Primary School

My Nan's Cat

Sacha is a chatty cat
He talks to Nan about this and that.

Although he's handsome
He's rather old
He stays inside out of the cold.

His silky fur is black and white
But he's a coward, too lazy to fight.

He sleeps all day
He sleeps all night
On his favourite blanket
Basked in warm sunlight.

And now it's the end
Of a beautiful day
He's going to take a nap
Goodnight.

Shannon Bett (9)
Wessex Primary School

The Weather

There's an almighty storm coming
Everyone's running
The lightning's coming down like an angry Zeus
It sounds like there is an angry wild bull on the loose
Hurricane or tornado nobody knows
It comes and it goes
Snow, rain or hail
It even could be a gale
Tidal wave or monsoon
It could happen soon
It's going to wreck a few towns
It's going to destroy the farmers' grounds
It's happening now
The dogs are giving a mighty growl.

Jack Brinsden (10)
Wessex Primary School

Spies - Haikus

Sneaky Spies

Some spies are sneaky,
They can unlock tricky codes,
Then they can break in.

Quiet Spies

Some spies are quiet,
They can sneak around the place,
Without being caught.

Clever Spies

Some spies are clever,
They can break into buildings
And steal their ideas.

Beni Grossman (9)
Wessex Primary School

What Can I See?

I am running through the rainforest, what can I see?
Plants and different species which I've never seen before.

I am climbing the mountain, what can I see?
Furious beasts and snoring dragons in the caves.

I am riding a camel in the desert, what can I see?
A mirage, a cactus and a charging rhino.

I am diving under the sea, what can I see?
Coral reefs and lots of species of fish.

I am hiking across the grassland, what can I see?
Trees, berry bushes and multicoloured birds.

I am walking in the ice lands, what can I see?
Packs of wolves and diving penguins.

I am limping through the canyons, what can I see?
I see nothing in the silence but plants.

I am driving through the city, what can I see?
The human race chatting and pets on leads.

I am finally at home, what can I see?
Michael Palin on my TV screen.

Matthew Sadlier (10)
Wessex Primary School

My English Teacher

I have an English teacher
She is very pretty
She is very sporty
She is 'Supergirl'
She is always saving my days
With her ideas
She runs up and down
She comes from Kent
She loves skiing through the wintry months
Her favourite subject is science
Her favourite colour is turquoise
She is really, really fun
She knows her French
She's a walking dictionary
Shes always wants to wear school uniform
My English teacher.

Layla Haigh-Ellery (9)
Wessex Primary School

The Silver Waterfall

Dashing through the forest
Gleaming in the sun
And when it reaches the bottom
It has so much fun.

It's as clear as ice
And rolls over rocks like a thousand dice.

Wild salmon dash through the cascades of silver water
Their pink scales flicker like stars
There are a million of them trapped in the waterfall
Rushing along like a fleet of cars.

When the water gets to the bottom it makes a big splash
And scares away all the fish with a big crash.

When the sun shines
It makes a new design.

Catherine Styles (10)
Wessex Primary School

Young Writers Information

We hope you have enjoyed reading this book - and that you will continue to enjoy it in the coming years.

If you like reading and writing poetry drop us a line, or give us a call, and we'll send you a free information pack.

Alternatively if you would like to order further copies of this book or any of our other titles, then please give us a call or log onto our website at
www.youngwriters.co.uk

Young Writers Information
Remus House
Coltsfoot Drive
Peterborough
PE2 9JX
(01733) 890066